SCHOLASTIC
News
Nonfiction Readers

D1532131

Neptune

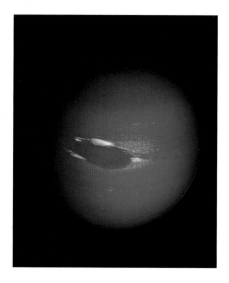

by
Melanie Chrismer

Children's Press
An Imprint of Scholastic Inc.
New York Toronto London Auckland Sydney
Mexico City New Delhi Hong Kong
Danbury, Connecticut

These content vocabulary word builders
are for grades 1–2.

Consultant: Michelle Yehling, Astronomy Education Consultant

Photo Credits:

Photographs © 2008: Bridgeman Art Library International Ltd., London/New York: 17 top (Lauros/Giraudon/Chateau de Versailles, France, by Felix Henri Giacomotti); Corbis Images/Hulton-Deutsch Collection: 17 bottom; NASA: back cover (JPL), cover, 2, 4 top, 5 bottom right, 5 top left, 7, 11, 19, 23 right; Photo Researchers, NY: 4 bottom right, 9 (Detlev van Ravenswaay), 4 bottom left, 5 bottom left, 15 (SPL); PhotoDisc/Getty Images via SODA: 1, 23 left, 23 top left.

Illustration Credits:

Illustration pages 5 top right, 13 by Pat Rasch

Illustrations on pages 20–21 by Greg Harris

Book Design: Simonsays Design!
Book Production: The Design Lab

Library of Congress Cataloging-in-Publication Data
Chrismer, Melanie.
Neptune / by Melanie Chrismer.—Updated ed.
    p. cm.—(Scholastic news nonfiction readers)
Includes bibliographical references and index.
ISBN-13: 978-0-531-14750-4 (lib. bdg.)   978-0-531-14765-8 (pbk.)
ISBN-10: 0-531-14750-9 (lib. bdg.)   0-531-14765-7 (pbk.)
1. Neptune (Planet)—Juvenile literature. I. Title.
QB691.C48 2007
523.48'1—dc22   2006102772

4 5 6 7 8 9 10 R 17 16 15 14 13 12 11

CONTENTS

WORD HUNT

Look for these words as you read. They will be in **bold**.

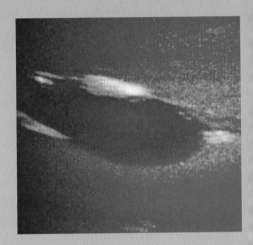

clouds
(kloudz)

scientists
(**sye**-uhn-tists)

solar system
(**soh**-lur **siss**-tuhm

4

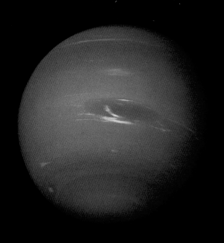

Neptune
(**nep**-toon)

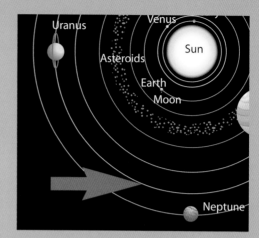

orbit
(**or**-bit)

telescope
(**tel**-uh-skope)

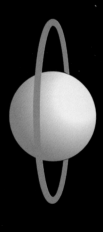

Uranus
(**yu**-rah-nuhss)

Neptune!

The planet **Neptune** looks blue.

It was named after Neptune, the Roman god of the sea.

Is there a sea of blue water on Neptune?

No. The blue color comes from the gas around the planet.

There is no water on Neptune.

Neptune is one of the biggest planets in our **solar system**.

Neptune is the eighth planet in our solar system.

All the planets in our solar system travel around the Sun on a path called an **orbit**.

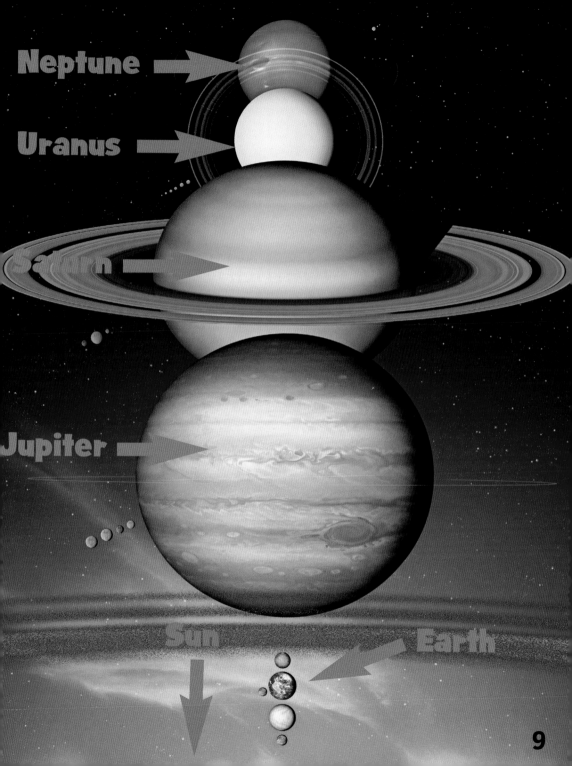

Neptune

Uranus

Saturn

Jupiter

Sun

Earth

9

Neptune is a big, cold, cloudy, windy planet.

Its **clouds** are made of a gas called methane.

Neptune also has the fastest winds of all the planets.

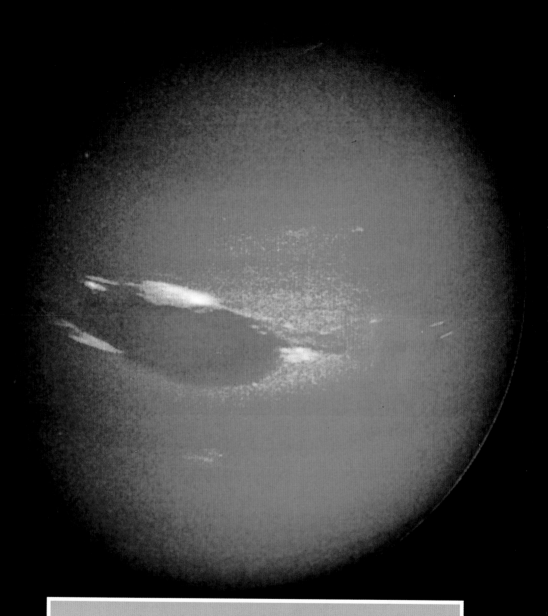

In some pictures of Neptune,
its clouds look pink.

Before **scientists** found Neptune, they were studying the planet **Uranus**.

They were surprised by its orbit.

Uranus did not follow the path they thought it would.

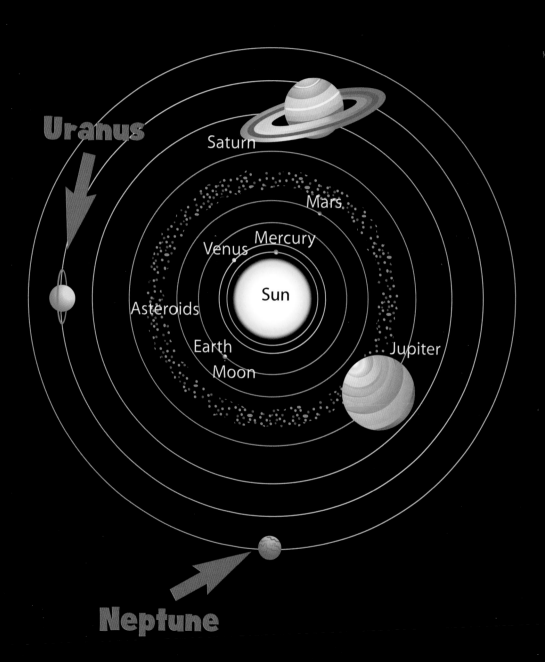

Uranus

Saturn

Mars

Venus

Mercury

Sun

Asteroids

Earth

Moon

Jupiter

Neptune

13

Scientists thought another planet was causing Uranus to travel in an unusual orbit.

They used math to figure out where the other planet might be.

Then astronomers used a **telescope** to look for it.

Telescopes are used to see things far away.

In 1846 the astronomers found the planet they were looking for.

They named it Neptune after the Roman god of the sea.

Urbain Le Verrier (top) and John Couch Adams (bottom) did the math to help discover Neptune.

Neptune was the first planet found using math.

Most of the other planets were found by watching the sky.

Who knows what other wonderful things will be found in space?

These pictures of Neptune were taken from the Hubble Space Telescope.

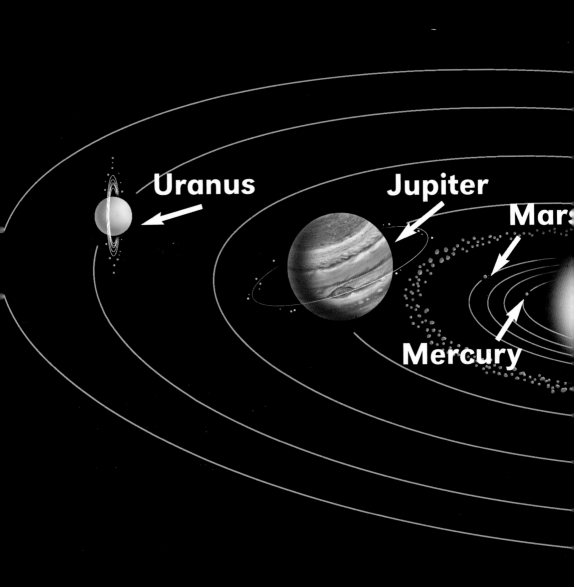

Uranus

Jupiter

Mars

Mercury

NEPTUNE
IN OUR SOLAR SYSTEM

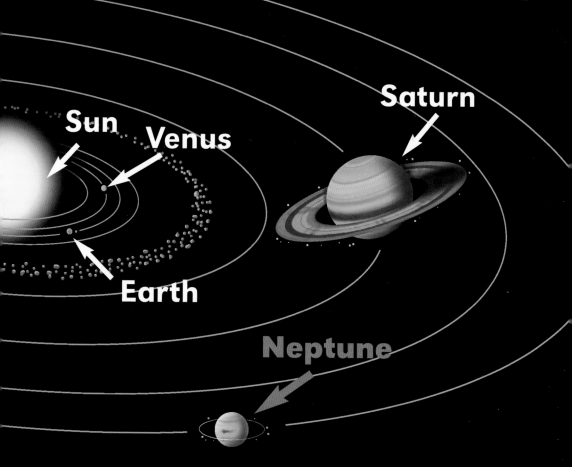

Sun

Venus

Saturn

Earth

Neptune

YOUR NEW WORDS

clouds (kloudz) groups of liquid droplets that can be seen above the surface of a planet

Neptune (**nep**-toon) a planet named after the Roman god of the sea

orbit (**or**-bit) the path an object takes around another object

scientists (**sye**-uhn-tists) people who study a subject by testing and observing

solar system (**soh**-lur **siss**-tuhm) the group of planets, moons, and other things that travel around the Sun

telescope (**tel**-uh-skope) a tool used to see things far away

Uranus (**yu**-rah-nuhss) the seventh planet

Earth and Neptune

A year is how long it takes a planet to go around the Sun.

 **1 Earth year
=365 days**

 **1 Neptune year
=60,225 Earth days
or 165 Earth years**

A day is how long it takes a planet to turn one time.

 **1 Earth day
= 24 hours**

 **1 Neptune day
= 16 Earth hours**

A moon is an object that circles a planet.

 **Earth has
1 moon.**

 **Neptune has
at least 13 moons
with more being
found all the time.**

**The winds on Neptune
can blow more than 1,200
miles (1,931 kilometers)
per hour.**

INDEX

FIND OUT MORE

Book:
Jenkins, Alvin. *Next Stop Neptune: Experiencing the Solar System.* Boston: Houghton Mifflin, 2004.

Web site:
Solar System Exploration
http://sse.jpl.nasa.gov/planets/

MEET THE AUTHOR

Melanie Chrismer grew up near NASA in Houston, Texas. She loves math and science and has written thirteen books for children. To write her books, she visited NASA where she floated in the zero-gravity trainer called the Vomit Comet. She says, "it is the best roller coaster ever!"